✳ ✳ ✳

700+ Insights to Mastering Short-Term Trading

※ ※ ※

700+ Insights to Mastering Short-Term Trading
Lifelong Lessons from a Seasoned Trader

Henrique M. Simões

Copyright © 2023 Henrique M. Simões
All rights reserved.

ISBN: 9798869782083

Table of Contents

1. Introduction..5
2. Essential Insights for Success..8
    2.1 The Trading Learning Curve...................................8
    2.2 The Power of Routine: Daily Habits for Traders..........12
    2.3 Essential Risk Management Insights........................15
    2.4 Hidden Wisdom..21
    2.5 Unveiling Trading Advantages Through Research........24
    2.6 Strategic Mindset: Winning the Trading Game............28

3. Essential Insights Unsorted..32
4. Enhancing Trading and Life through Non-Trading Beliefs....134
5. Appendix I: Journey to Profits......................................139
Glossary...141
About the Author...152

* * *
Chapter 1

"What we call 'mastery' is the mysterious process through which what is at first difficult or even impossible becomes easy and pleasurable through diligent, patient, long-term practice."

-- George Leonard

"I work too damn hard to accept mediocre results."

-- Paul Tudor Jones

Introduction

Why did I write this book? Ever since I was young, my big dream was to become a successful trader. I never thought about any other job or direction in life; I always felt that pull. But I never realized that the path to success would be so long, narrow, and difficult to navigate. To be a successful trader who can rely solely on trading to make a living, you have to relentlessly strive for perfection. Sometimes, you need to work on competitive advantages, trading setups, and systems, while other times, you need to focus on risk management, motivation, mindset, or even the organization and planning of the business.

And that's where the idea to write this book came from—to cover all the topics I encountered throughout my journey of development. Written in this concise way, it allows traders to flip through the pages and find the message that might be exactly what they need at a specific stage of their development. I encourage you to use this book as a practical guide, taking notes in the margins and underlining the relevant parts.

In the book's second chapter, trading insights are categorized into six focal points: mastering the trading learning curve, leveraging the impact of trading routines, essential insights into risk management, the nuanced wisdom exclusive to seasoned traders, market testing and research, and a comprehensive exploration of the intricate mind game involved in trading.

The third chapter stands as the book's cornerstone. Within its pages, you'll uncover insights tied to subjects explored in various sections of the second chapter, along with many others directly or indirectly pertinent to cultivating a robust trading performance. In this chapter, all topics are interwoven, prompting readers to skim through diverse insights and concentrate on what aligns with their needs at a given moment. The underlying rationale for amalgamating all trading insights into a unified reservoir lies in the acknowledgment that, while seeking guidance on a specific topic, one may unexpectedly discover another relevant insight suitable for their current trading needs or developmental stage.

In the fourth chapter of the book, I've elaborated on some ideas and non-trading beliefs that I deem essential for achieving success in this business.

Enjoy your reading!

***
Chapter 2

Essential Insights for Success

2.1 The Trading Learning Curve: The Path to Proficiency and Success

The "trading learning curve" refers to the process and journey that individuals go through as they acquire the knowledge, skills, and experience necessary to become proficient and successful traders. It involves a series of stages, challenges, and milestones that traders typically encounter as they gain a better understanding of financial markets, develop trading strategies, learn risk management techniques, and become more adept at controlling their emotions. The learning curve can vary from trader to trader and encompasses both successes and setbacks, ultimately leading to improved trading performance and consistency over time.

- People often underestimate the time required to become a profitable trader.

- Great traders are made, not born; they evolve with time.

- Set real expectations; fast riches won't come.

- The novice trader's fatal flaw is to experience success on their initial trade.

- The first successful trade can be a trap for beginner traders, as it can give a false sense of confidence and lead to poor decision-making in subsequent trades.

- The key to success in any endeavor, including trading, is having the desire, the right knowledge, and the determination to keep going.

- Reading about trading builds a foundation, but mastery comes from practical application of knowledge.

- The more you read about trading, the more you may feel like you're in a never-ending maze of information.

- Trading, like sex, is best learned through practice rather than theory.

- Mastery isn't achieved through passive learning; it demands reflection, practice, and real-world application of knowledge.

- Seek proximity to prosperous traders for enhanced success.

- Trading isn't like a science where you can easily copy success from one person to another. It's more like an art, and the best traders are like skilled artists.

- If you trade for thrills or bragging, treat account money as entertainment expense.

- Successful trading requires creativity, and the most accomplished traders, much like exceptional artists, enthusiastically embrace their uniqueness.

- The best way to learn trading is by doing it.

- You won't truly understand the complexities and nuances of trading until you've experienced it firsthand.

- Cultivating oneself in broader areas such as psychology and behavior is just as crucial as studying the markets.

- As a small independent trader, you have an inherent advantage. Smaller traders can operate unnoticed, making market moves without affecting prices.

- While complexity often provides institutions with their competitive advantage, simplicity is where retail traders discover their edge.

- To attain proficiency as a trader and generate stable income is an acquirable expertise.

- Trading's real challenge is finding an edge, yet staying emotionally resilient and committed to your system amid underperformance or losses.

- The majority of traders cannot withstand the learning curve. Once things become challenging, and the inevitable drawdown appears, they start seeking other options.

- Mistakes lead to experience, reducing the chance of repetition through subconscious learning.

- Your passion for the markets will pave the way to your success.

- Paper trading can't fully prepare you for the real market's emotional and financial pressures.

- Paper trading is beneficial for practicing execution and getting familiar with a new trading platform.

- Experience is the bare minimum requirement for success in trading.

- Copying others won't yield lasting success.

- Trading is a long game, requiring a deep understanding of the markets and oneself.

- Success demands a minimum level of experience, knowledge, and skill.

- Properly exploring financial markets leads to a better life, freedom, and independence.

- The greats in any field are always learning.

- The journey to consistent trading is tough, but the rewards make it worthwhile: financial gains and personal fulfillment.

2.2 The Power of Routine: Daily Habits for Traders

Cultivating a disciplined and effective trading routine is vital for traders looking to optimize performance. Here are key elements of a robust daily trading regimen:

- A pre-trading walk clears the mind, reduces stress, and enhances focus. It promotes blood flow, boosts energy.

- Have water at your desk, stay hydrated, and keep your focus. Dehydration results in mistakes and poor trades.

- Start your computer and trading platform well in advance. A few times a year, login issues may arise, and you might not be able to resolve them in time.

- Begin the day by reviewing the news and economic calendar to be aware of any market-moving events.

- Calculate the position size for each trade to align with your risk management strategy.

- Keep your trading journal open at all times, and make daily entries. It's a crucial tool for tracking and understanding your trading actions.

- Get a notebook, jot down market observations; it sparks ideas and helps you cultivate trading habits.

- Don't take your losses home; leave them in the market. Return the next day with renewed focus and dedication to trading effectively.

- Execute trades, monitor, and assess your performance.

- Staring at prices all day is like constantly feeding a slot machine.

- When trading different strategies, use separate accounts.

- Avoid setting daily profit targets and focus on long-term performance goals for greater consistency.

- Always review your trading day. Note down what you did well and where you went wrong, then plan your next trading session accordingly.

- Get ready for the trading session the night before.

- Perform a post-session analysis: record trades, assess strengths, and identify areas for improvement.

- Fuel your enthusiasm through post-market research.

- Avoid the inclination to incessantly monitor your account balance.

- Allocate time for researching the markets regularly.

- Tracking your trading activities leads to growth and better results.

- Perform a post-session analysis: record trades, assess strengths, and identify areas for improvement.

- Practice mindfulness, meditation, or stress-reduction techniques to maintain emotional stability during trading.

2.3 Essential Risk Management Insights

Effective risk management is a cornerstone of short-term trading success. It safeguards your capital, vital in a field marked by rapid market shifts. By setting limits on individual trade risk, you ensure the longevity of your trading activities. Furthermore, it instills consistency and predictability, enabling better evaluation and ongoing improvement of your trading strategies. Here are some insights on effectively managing risk in short-term trading:

- Determine the appropriate position size to limit exposure to a specific trade relative to your overall account size.

- Implement stop-loss orders to automatically exit a trade if it moves against you beyond a predefined point, limiting potential losses.

- Use take-profit orders to lock in profits when a trade reaches a certain favorable level, preventing potential reversals.

- Avoid over-concentration in a single asset or trade; diversify your portfolio to spread risk.

- Consider the historical and implied volatility of assets to adjust position sizes and risk tolerance accordingly.

- Continuously monitor open positions and adjust stop-loss and take-profit levels if market conditions change.

- Stay informed about upcoming economic events, earnings reports, or news releases that could impact your positions.

- Develop a well-defined trading plan with rules and guidelines for entry, exit, and risk management.

- Prioritize the preservation of your trading capital over aggressive profit-seeking.

- Practice risk management strategies in a simulated trading environment before using real capital.

- Be aware of correlations between assets in your portfolio to avoid overexposure to similar risk factors.

- Exercise caution when using leverage, as it can amplify both gains and losses; ensure you fully understand its implications.

- Regularly assess your risk tolerance and adjust your trading approach accordingly, especially after significant wins or losses.

- Have contingency plans for unexpected events, such as flash crashes or sudden market news, to limit potential damage.

- Understand the difference between market orders (which execute immediately) and limit orders (which execute at a specified price), and use them accordingly in managing risk.

- Periodically review and refine your risk management strategies based on your trading performance and market conditions.

- Conduct thorough analysis before entering a trade to ensure it aligns with your risk management goals.

- Be prepared to act swiftly when your predetermined risk thresholds are reached, without emotional hesitation.

- Diversify your trading strategies and systems to spread risk. Utilizing multiple trading systems can aid in minimizing the impact of unfavorable market conditions on your overall portfolio.

- When you risk a fixed amount of trading capital per trade, like 1%, you become indifferent to any specific trade, which allows you to make objective decisions without being influenced by emotions.

- Novice traders often engage in excessively large trades.

- When you catch yourself praying over a position, it's time to liquidate it immediately.

- If you find yourself in a state of panic, your position is simply too large for you to handle.

- Avoid rushing to recover lost terrain at a single stroke.

- A single reckless trade can erase months of effort. It's the thing that sets back many traders I've known.

- A trader must minimize losses and grow equity over time.

- Adapt to accepting small, managed losses. Regard them as essential steps, not disappointments.

- Your trading success starts the day you accept that losing in a trade is something normal.

- Only invest what you can afford to lose without sacrificing your peace of mind.

- Drawdowns are as inevitable as death itself.

- Set predefined drawdown limits to determine if a system is not performing as expected and should be discontinued.

- As a trader, your objective should be to maintain a smooth and upward-sloping equity curve.

- Prepare for the unexpected, as bad luck is ever-present. Survival hinges on planning for its arrival.

- Traders should exercise restraint when contemplating significant and sudden increases in their trading size.

- Speculative markets are inherently uncertain and cannot be fully understood.

- Escaping excessive risks is vital for successful trading.

- The temptation to recoup all of your losses in a single trade is a recipe for failure in the markets.

- Accepting 8 to 10 consecutive trading losses yearly is essential; safeguard your account during these times.

- You must be mindful that a very bad trade can wipe out months or even years of profits.

- Once you have a winning system in place and adhere to wise risk management, the only thing left to conquer is your own mentality.

- The path to ruin in trading is paved with the decision to keep adding to a losing position.

- Limiting losses: The vital cornerstone of trading.

- Avoid setting daily profit targets and focus on long-term performance goals for greater consistency.

- Avoid the detrimental mental state of believing the market owes you something after consecutive losses.

- It's possible to experience a day of losses while still ending the week with profits.

- Steer clear of scenarios where risk cannot be effectively managed.

2.4 Hidden Wisdom: Insights Known Only to Seasoned, Exceptional Traders

There's a specific type of knowledge that is intrinsic to learning. It is only those who have skin in the game for a certain period of time and wholeheartedly dedicate themselves to a particular activity who discover nuances about the nature of the business that others can't even fathom. Here are a few of them that I consider highly relevant.

- Great traders are made, not born; they evolve with time.

- Strive to connect with seasoned and trustworthy traders, individuals who have forged a path of consistent success.

- Almost every great trader, if not all, suffered a catastrophic loss, depleting their trading account. It is an integral part of their journey.

- Better to learn the harsh lesson of losing it all with small capital than to face it later with a fortune on the line.

- A losing trade shouldn't disturb you.

- Focus on doing more of what works and less of what doesn't.

- Escaping excessive risks is vital for successful trading.

- The key to success in any endeavor, including trading, is having the desire, the right knowledge, and the determination to keep going.

- While complexity often provides institutions with their competitive advantage, simplicity is where retail traders discover their edge.

- Trading can become addictive. Strive to maintain a sense of balance in your life.

- Be well-prepared; rivals are.

- To make money in trading, an organized trading plan is essential.

- The objective clarity you possess before entering a trade quickly dissipates once you're in it.

- Successful traders are those who commit to a specific style and remain consistent with it.

- It's the edge that sets you apart and attracts the money.

- Belief in the positive nature of money is crucial for accumulating wealth.

- Cultivating oneself in broader areas such as psychology and behavior is just as crucial as studying the markets.

- Prepare for the unexpected, as bad luck is ever-present. Survival hinges on planning for its arrival.

- With skillful execution, a small trading advantage can yield immense wealth.

- In trading, simplicity is the ultimate sophistication.

- Trade within your emotional capacity; avoid taking positions larger than you can handle.

- To counteract doubt and uncertainty in the markets, develop a systematic trading process.

- Impeccable work ethic yields remarkable rewards.

- Successful traders seldom have an effortless journey, except when they hail from a family of traders.

- Learn from your trades; the sole path to progress.

- In trading, the impossible happens approximately twice a year.

- Making sound trading decisions becomes challenging when you're tired or stressed.

- While science provides valuable inputs, trading is an art form.

- Financial markets are made by people, and there's no secret physics code hidden in them.

2.5 Unveiling Trading Advantages Through Research

The most effective way to gain a competitive edge in trading, enabling consistent profits in the financial markets, is through idea testing using historical price series and evaluating how a specific asset behaves under conditions predefined by the researcher. The study of price patterns, trends, and technical indicators in specific contexts is crucial to empower the trader with statistical confidence. I share with you some pertinent observations on this topic.

- The ability to quantify and test ideas is vital for successful trading.

- When starting out, a good approach is to focus on learning and understanding how a trend system operates.

- Observe and then test 'What if' scenarios. When a particular event occurs, what typically follows? This is an excellent method for discovering your trading advantage.

- When designing trading systems, simplicity consistently outperforms complexity. Statistically, simplicity proves to be more reliable than complexity.

- A short-term trading system can only handle a certain amount of money while remaining profitable.

- Skilled traders pose insightful questions, which drive effective market research.

- Set predefined drawdown limits to determine if a system is not performing as expected and should be discontinued.

- The Profit Factor is the ultimate metric for ranking trading strategies, measuring dollar inflow versus dollar outflow.

- Quantify every element of your trading. Measurement leads to progress.

- In trading, an unsuccessful backtest serves as a signal pointing in a different direction.

- Proper backtesting requires a deep understanding of the market and experience. Beginners often overlook important details that can lead to costly mistakes.

- Resist the temptation to alter a trading system merely due to a few consecutive losing trades.

- You can have the best system in the world, but if you don't execute flawlessly, it won't matter.

- Craft a system tailored to a specific market; if it proves effective, consider adapting it to other markets. Remember, each market possesses distinct dynamics, rhythms, and personalities.

- The path to discovering an edge is to locate entry points with a probability greater than average of the market moving in the desired direction within a specific timeframe.

- From a couple of hundred backtests, only one or two may demonstrate effectiveness and be applied to real-money trading.

- Edges are small, execution is everything, and the line between success and failure is razor-thin.

- Following backtesting and confirming promise on historical data, proceed to forward test the trading system using live price feeds. Only after successful forward testing should you consider deploying your funds into it.

- Fine-tuning optimization is often a futile effort or even self-deception.

- Optimization's value lies in setting broad parameter boundaries for a system.

- Through backtesting experience, you'll grasp market subtleties, guiding future research. The longer you test, the more familiar you become with market tendencies.

- The more you test, the greater the chance for good luck to intervene, as you have more opportunities to encounter something that aligns well with the market you are studying.

- Evaluate the robustness of your trading system by comparing short-term metrics with their long-term counterparts.

2.6 Strategic Mindset: Winning the Trading Game

The mental aspect of trading is the final and most challenging battle to conquer. The need to win, self-sabotage, internal conflicts in the individual's relationship with money, and the aversion or inclination to risk are immense variables that, collectively, have a more profound impact on the ultimate outcome than even the methodology itself. Here are some of the most crucial observations on this intricate and majestic topic:

- Errors from self-sabotage arise from inner conflicts about deserving money or victory.

- Self-sabotage often stems from feeling unworthy of success.

- Disorganized and impatient traders lose.

- To succeed in trading, you must realize that you are responsible for the outcome.

- In trading, discipline is not merely a virtue but a necessity.

- To be successful, focus on the big picture and don't worry too much about what happens in each trade.

- The two most perilous expressions in trading are: *"I think"* and *"I feel"*. Avoid depending on personal judgments and emotions. Opt for a systematic approach instead.

- Your passion for the markets will pave the way to your success.

- Don't touch a stock or future that spooks you. Your instincts are warning you for a reason.

- If trading doesn't make you happy, maybe you're forcing yourself into it instead of doing what you're truly passionate, talented, and skilled at.

- Your trading success starts the day you accept that losing in a trade is something normal.

- After reaching a specific monetary goal, some traders struggle to maintain their successful discipline.

- Avoid the inclination to incessantly monitor your account balance.

- The fascinating thing about successful trading is that the right behaviors begin as written rules and evolve into habits.

- A losing trade shouldn't disturb you.

- Becoming fixated on market analysis may create a perception of certitude.

- Strong motivation is a shared trait among high achievers, including successful traders.

- To minimize the significance of a single trade, focus on the net outcome of the next ten or twenty trades.

- Trading is a competition; ignite the competitor within you.

- Trade within your emotional capacity; avoid taking positions larger than you can handle.

- Belief in the positive nature of money is crucial for accumulating wealth.

- The presence of stress in trading is an indicator that something is not quite right.

- Traders, like athletes, must have a winning attitude to succeed.

- You can have the best system in the world, but if you don't execute flawlessly, it won't matter.

- When armed with a winning system and a measured approach to risk management, the only obstacle is your mindset.

- It's not finding the statistical advantage that's tough, but being emotionally stable and consistent in capitalizing on it.

- In the realm of long-term trading success, there's no psychological trait more crucial than resilience.

* * *
Chapter 3

Essential Insights Unsorted

This chapter encompasses topics suitable for traders at all levels of development. The reason the insights are not presented in a specific order is simple. My intention was to enable the reader to flow freely among insights on multiple relevant topics. Sometimes, we focus on improving one aspect of our trading while neglecting others that also demand our urgent attention. This approach allows the reader to navigate Chapter Three freely, with a pencil in hand, underlining and annotating sections that are currently areas of focus.

Even as a trader achieves consistent profitability, there are ongoing areas for improvement—such as scaling trading size without affecting performance, achieving a balance between work and family life, and examining beliefs about the nature of money.

This book also caters to my personal needs, allowing me to carry it everywhere, open it to any page, and jot down notes on specific subjects I aim to tackle at any given moment. Let's dive in:

$

Properly exploring financial markets leads to a better life, freedom, and independence.

$

Great traders are made, not born; they evolve with time.

$

Getting good at trading takes a long time and you'll face setbacks. Be prepared for that.

$

You're competing with individuals who have dedicated a significant part of their lives to the same pursuit.

$

The key to success in any endeavor, including trading, is having the desire, the right knowledge, and the determination to keep going.

$

Trading can become addictive. Strive to maintain a sense of balance in your life.

$

Mastery isn't achieved through passive learning; it demands reflection, practice, and real-world application of knowledge.

$

As a small independent trader, you have an inherent advantage. Smaller traders can operate unnoticed, making market moves without affecting prices.

$

While complexity often provides institutions with their competitive advantage, simplicity is where retail traders discover their edge.

$

Markets exhibit repetition. At its core, trading is about recognizing and navigating these repetitive patterns. With increased trading experience, identifying and trading these patterns becomes more effortless.

$

Observe and then test 'What if' scenarios. When a particular event occurs, what typically follows? This is an excellent method for discovering your trading advantage.

$

When designing trading systems, simplicity consistently outperforms complexity. Statistically, simplicity proves to be more reliable than complexity.

$

Set real expectations; fast riches won't come.

$

A short-term trading system can only handle a certain amount of money while remaining profitable.

$

The best way to learn trading is by doing it.

$

Successful trading requires creativity, and the most accomplished traders, much like exceptional artists, enthusiastically embrace their uniqueness.

$

Practice and experience are the best teachers in trading.

$

Don't dwell on your trading errors; they're a part of every journey. Absorb the lesson, stride forward - fast.

$

People often underestimate the time required to become a profitable trader.

$

Reading about trading builds a foundation, but mastery comes from practical application of knowledge.

$

If you trade for thrills or bragging, treat account money as entertainment expense.

$

The less you depend on a trade for profit, the higher your chances of allowing the market to work its way to profitability.

$

The ability to discern when to refrain from trading is a skill in its own right.

$

Trading isn't like a science where you can easily copy success from one person to another. It's more like an art, and the best traders are like skilled artists.

$

Disorganized and impatient traders lose.

$

In trading, you'll encounter both wins and losses. However, the combined outcome should reflect your inherent advantage, visible in a rising equity curve.

$

Errors from self-sabotage arise from inner conflicts about deserving money or victory.

$

Be well-prepared; rivals are.

$

Self-sabotage often stems from feeling unworthy of success.

$

The first successful trade can be a trap for beginner traders, as it can give a false sense of confidence and lead to poor decision-making in subsequent trades.

$

When starting out, a good approach is to focus on learning and understanding how a trend system operates.

$

Seek proximity to prosperous traders for enhanced success.

$

First, you'll become good at specific trades before mastering trading as a whole.

$

Your trading failures are visible in your equity curve.

$

The equity curve is a merciless judge of your trading performance.

$

Every trader, knowingly or not, embodies an entrepreneur. They establish their business and compete within the trading marketplace alongside their peers.

$

Every trader's objective is to make money regularly.

$

Only the equity curve provides a clear and honest reflection of your success and failures.

$

The novice trader's fatal flaw is to experience success on their initial trade.

$

Mastery of a chosen approach, not its specifics, leads the superior trader to greatness in trading.

$

In trading, discipline is not merely a virtue but a necessity.

$

The key to successful trading lies in realizing your responsibility for the results you achieve. Winners embrace it, while losers evade it.

$

A single reckless trade can erase months of effort. It's the thing that sets back many traders I've known.

$

Avoid rushing to recover lost terrain at a single stroke.

$

Trading is a form of entrepreneurship, where the success or failure of your business is reflected in your equity curve.

$

Smart people who embrace and learn from their mistakes outperform their equally capable counterparts who lack such openness.

$

You won't truly understand the complexities and nuances of trading until you've experienced it firsthand.

$

Trading discipline is the starting point, but it is the ongoing maintenance of discipline that propels us towards progress.

$

Trading, like sex, is best learned through practice rather than theory.

$

The more you read about trading, the more you may feel like you're in a never-ending maze of information.

$

To win in trading, you need more than just an opinion.

$

To succeed in trading, you must realize that you are responsible for the outcome.

$

Trading success demands acceptance of personal accountability.

$

If you incorporate external information to decide whether to act on a signal, you introduce unpredictable elements to your trading advantage.

$

Trading discipline is the foundation upon which progress is built.

$

When you catch yourself praying over a position, it's time to liquidate it immediately.

$

Trading discipline is the foundation upon which progress is built.

$

With every step forward, discipline remains the key to success.

$

Successful traders are those who commit to a specific style and remain consistent with it.

$

The temptation to drift from one approach to another can be great, but it rarely pays off in the end.

$

Skilled traders pose insightful questions, which drive effective market research.

$

The objective clarity you possess before entering a trade quickly dissipates once you're in it.

$

To trade effectively, plan your trade and execute your plan.

$

The two most perilous expressions in trading are: *"I think"* and *"I feel"*. Avoid depending on personal judgments and emotions. Opt for a systematic approach instead.

$

Being an elite trader is a special talent, but anyone can learn to be a skilled trader and earn money consistently.

$

To attain proficiency as a trader and generate stable income is an acquirable expertise.

$

Master consistency in trading, and watch it transform your entire life.

$

Profitable trading isn't about being correct; it's about executing trades effectively.

$

To be successful, focus on the big picture and don't worry too much about what happens in each trade.

$

In trading, money moves like a river. It flows away from the ones with mere opinions and towards the ones with a clear edge.

$

A true pro trader remains within their circle of expertise, dismissing all else.

$

In trading, you can always control when you trade and how much you bet.

$

Avoid doubling your position near the initial entry point, especially after being in a profitable position.

$

In trading, it's tough to accept a small loss and resist taking a small profit too soon.

$

After a profitable streak in the markets, taking a few days off is crucial.

$

The quality of a trader's active hours is defined by the time and effort invested in refining their trading system when the markets are closed.

$

Poor trades often stem from the impulse to take action.

$

The markets are an ever-evolving beast, forever transforming and changing.

$

Mentors at trading firms often advise keeping a trading journal on the desk—an effective way to track and understand our actions.

$

It's the edge that sets you apart and attracts the money.

$

Trading is like a game of tug-of-war. The money is the rope, and the ones with an edge always end up pulling it towards them.

$

Think of markets like living beings. Watch one market every day for a month. Get to know it, and it will show you where it wants to go.

$

The art of profitable speculation is the most demanding profession that necessitates a combination of hard work, intelligence, patience, and mental discipline.

$

What worked yesterday might not work today, and what works today might not work tomorrow.

$

Probabilities in trading are shaped by historical patterns, excluding potential future events.

$

To excel, your strategy must be dynamic, constantly evolving, requiring continuous learning and adaptation.

$

The moment you become complacent, your downfall begins.

$

Be humble as a trader, never assume you're infallible.

$

If trading doesn't make you happy, maybe you're forcing yourself into it instead of doing what you're truly passionate, talented, and skilled at.

$

Your passion for the markets will pave the way to your success.

$

Novice traders often engage in excessively large trades.

$

Trading is an exhilarating experience that brings a sense of vitality and a deeper understanding of life.

$

A bad trading day can feel like a punch in the gut.

$

No proper setup, no trade. Recognizing when to stay out of the markets is just as crucial as knowing when to participate.

$

Quality trading requires careful examination of both market dynamics and your own performance. A process-driven trader doesn't blindly follow routines but identifies effective strategies, comprehends them, and consistently improves execution.

$

The market is not the true enemy of the trader; it is the inner self that must be conquered.

$

Your trading success starts the day you accept that losing in a trade is something normal.

$

Don't take your losses home; leave them in the market. Return the next day with renewed focus and dedication to trading effectively.

$

The convergence of inexperience, youth, and limited capital is why many traders face consistent losses on their path.

$

Highly effective traders intentionally embrace uniqueness, approaching the market in their own special way. They notice things others miss, developing a unique perspective for understanding the markets.

$

A trader must minimize losses and grow equity over time.

$

Always review your trading day. Note down what you did well and where you went wrong, then plan your next trading session accordingly.

$

Execute trades, monitor, and assess your performance.

$

Refusing to acknowledge mistakes is the gravest trading error, hindering your potential for improvement.

$

When trading different strategies, use separate accounts.

$

Incorporate breaks strategically during trading—use a random alarm as a reminder to assess your mental readiness. Ensure you're in the right mindset for effective trading.

$

To beat the traders in your market and timeframe, be better prepared than them.

$

The analogy between snipers and traders highlights the value of discipline and patience in achieving success.

$

Trading's real challenge is finding an edge, yet staying emotionally resilient and committed to your system amid underperformance or losses.

$

When you risk a fixed amount of trading capital per trade, like 1%, you become indifferent to any specific trade, which allows you to make objective decisions without being influenced by emotions.

$

Successful traders, like snipers, prioritize preparation and practice before engaging in their field of expertise.

$

Get ready for the trading session the night before.

$

Expertise in trading, like sniping, requires the ability to maintain composure and focus under pressure.

$

Avoid the common mistake of becoming less disciplined after a successful trading period.

$

The required discipline to become an effective and prosperous trader is possessed by only a small percentage of individuals.

$

Trading philosophy is earned through personal experience, effort, and learning from mistakes; it cannot be borrowed or taught directly.

$

Cultivating oneself in broader areas such as psychology and behavior is just as crucial as studying the markets.

$

The true best traders don't ponder over the amount of time they devote to their trading business.

$

Don't waste your capital on suboptimal trades. You'll be too weak to capitalize on the right ones.

$

Quality trading requires careful examination of both market dynamics and your own performance. A process-driven trader doesn't blindly follow routines but identifies effective strategies, comprehends them, and consistently improves execution.

$

Consistency outweighs high profits in a system. A steady edge across trades ensures a smooth equity curve and leveraged gains. Gauge system stability by comparing key metrics over varying time spans.

$

If trading were a science, success could replicate across people. Trading, though, it's an art, and the true masters are artists.

$

Financial markets are made by people, and there's no secret physics code hidden in them.

$

Sitting at a desk all day, staring at the markets, can lead you to do things out of sheer boredom that you don't truly desire.

$

Without cash, the trading business cannot thrive.

$

The more you think about and practice your trading rules, the more they become a natural part of you.

$

Don't overtrade. It can be just as detrimental to your trading as holding onto losing positions for too long.

$

Improve your trading by trading less, watching markets closely, and recording observations. This approach accelerates progress and provides insights for future testing and implementation.

$

In trading, you must be both defensive and aggressive at the same time.

$

Learning what should be done in trading is simpler than putting it into practice. Successful trading principles often defy typical human inclinations.

$

Traders abandon the learning curve, fleeing at difficulty and drawdown, seeking alternatives.

$

The majority of traders cannot withstand the learning curve. Once things become challenging, and the inevitable drawdown appears, they start seeking other options.

$

To excel in trading, you must master one methodology instead of being mildly proficient in various trading styles.

$

True trading mastery requires the whole of a person.

$

You need to be aggressive in pursuing profits and defensive in protecting them.

$

Traders face their toughest challenge when enticed by the alluring temptation of breaking their rules for immediate profits, which may yield short-term gains but ultimately leads to long-term losses.

$

Among those who grasp the basics, only a minority shall triumph as accomplished traders.

$

In times of loss, the key is to trust your methods.

$

Only a trader fully committed to the craft can master the markets.

$

After reaching a specific monetary goal, some traders struggle to maintain their successful discipline.

$

Cash is key for traders. It is their inventory, lifeline, and best friend. No cash, no business.

$

Perform a post-session analysis: record trades, assess strengths, and identify areas for improvement.

$

The market is indifferent to you, unaffected by your gains or losses.

$

The market is an objective force that operates beyond our control.

$

The cumulative outcome of your trading endeavors, spanning numerous trades, shall be determined by the effectiveness of your trading system, less any errors in your execution.

$

Mistakes lead to experience, reducing the chance of repetition through subconscious learning.

$

Success in trading comes from finding your niche.

$

Losers often delay accepting losses until they jeopardize their trading business.

$

Emotional toughness is a byproduct of understanding your approach and its performance over time.

$

Drawdowns are as inevitable as death itself.

$

To embark on the path of a trader, one must gracefully weather short-term discomforts in pursuit of enduring long-term gains.

$

Have faith in your methods to withstand the storm of losses.

$

Trading is a give-and-take game: you'll experience losses and wins, and it's essential to handle both with a positive attitude.

$

Discovering market success and personal compatibility takes time and patience.

$

Superior traders identify a niche that aligns with their psychology, time zone, market preference, account size, and specific trading hours, and dedicate themselves to mastering that niche.

$

The extroverted trader embodies aggression, competitiveness, and a relentless drive to excel in the field.

$

Trading is a long game, requiring a deep understanding of the markets and oneself.

$

You should avoid making sudden, unplanned trades.

$

Emotional strength arises from understanding your method's long-term performance and embracing inevitable drawdowns.

$

Only by staying the course can one achieve lasting success.

$

Fuel your enthusiasm through post-market research.

$

Prepare for the unexpected, as bad luck is ever-present. Survival hinges on planning for its arrival.

$

Trading encompasses both introverted and extroverted elements.

$

The trader's external persona portrays a relentless, ambitious individual, always striving to be the best in the field.

$

Swiftly forget losses.

$

Regardless of the trading strategy employed, containing losses surpasses half the battle.

$

Avoid the inclination to incessantly monitor your account balance.

$

The trader's introverted nature emerges as a disciplined, solitary workaholic.

$

Financial constraints hinder profitable trading.

$

Discover your strengths and shape strategies that revolve around them.

$

As a professional trader reliant on trading for a living, prioritize a trading approach that fosters steady equity growth over sporadic bursts.

$

Caution: Large positions have a tendency to manipulate your emotions.

$

When winning, beware of overconfidence leading to errors like unclear entry signals or excessive position sizing.

$

Traders should exercise restraint when contemplating significant and sudden increases in their trading size.

$

Consistent income is vital for a pro trader.

$

Exercise restraint when trading the market; handle it delicately, or it may harm you.

$

Losses are an unavoidable part of the journey.

$

Traders often excel with smaller positions but struggle with larger ones, even in highly liquid markets.

$

In the realm of trading, embracing discomfort and imperfections is crucial. Success in trading stems from this acceptance; holding a different perspective only results in frustration and disappointment.

$

Money flows in and out. Every strategy encompasses both winning and losing trades.

$

A top trader thrives through comprehensive market study.

$

Mean reversion trading exhibits superior performance when applied to trading instruments characterized by heightened liquidity and a well-established, mature status.

$

Learn to cherish your downtime and find joy beyond the markets.

$

Indulging in foolish mistakes can initiate a self-perpetuating cycle. Avoid falling into that perilous trap.

$

When trading becomes an overwhelming struggle, extricate your mind from the chaos.

$

The success rate of trades holds minimal significance as a performance metric.

$

Investing in knowledge always yields returns.

$

Predicting the direction of a market at any given time is impossible with certainty.

$

Some traders abandon winning systems at the first sign of underperformance, succumbing to a critical error.

$

Ensure your strategy remains adaptable to evolving market conditions, allowing for necessary adjustments when needed.

$

Enhance your understanding of market dynamics by analyzing your trading losses.

$

Allocate time for researching the markets regularly.

$

The longer it takes for a trade to turn profitable, the higher the likelihood of it ending in a loss.

$

In moments of winning, the risk of committing overconfident trading errors arises.

$

Trusting in a trading guru is a shortcut that leads to dependency. Self-mastery is the only path to true success.

$

Relying solely on a trading guru is a recipe for disaster.

$

Never become excessively confident in a single trade. Regardless of a promising setup, any trade can result in losses. Instead, place your confidence in your strategy and methodology.

$

The foundation of a trader's enduring wealth accumulation is grounded in steadfast trust in their own dependability.

$

A top trader thrives through comprehensive market study.

$

Avoid obsessing over the value of your trading account throughout the day.

$

Remember, you are competing with highly intelligent people who have devoted their lives to this field. Do not expect it to be a smooth ride.

$

Every market is constantly evolving, and any trading method must undergo ongoing refinement.

$

The ability to quantify and test ideas is vital for successful trading.

$

In trading, an unsuccessful backtest serves as a signal pointing in a different direction.

$

It proves beneficial to classify a market using the following pairs: calm or volatile, trending or consolidating.

$

As a trader, your objective should be to maintain a smooth and upward-sloping equity curve.

$

Speculative markets are inherently uncertain and cannot be fully understood.

$

If you find yourself in a state of panic, your position is simply too large for you to handle.

$

Self-control and a winning methodology stand on equal ground, each indispensable.

$

Even the most promising trade can end in loss. There are no guarantees in the markets.

$

Acknowledge your humanity and the inevitability of making mistakes. Practice self-forgiveness.

$

Good traders refrain from making impulsive decisions.

$

Averaging losses is a common error among inexperienced traders.

$

Better to learn the harsh lesson of losing it all with small capital than to face it later with a fortune on the line.

$

Incompetent traders often fall victim to the grave error of averaging losses, compounding their misfortune and veering further off course.

$

Almost every great trader, if not all, suffered a catastrophic loss, depleting their trading account. It is an integral part of their journey.

$

With skillful execution, a small trading advantage can yield immense wealth.

$

Fear fuels trading mistakes.

$

Quantify every element of your trading. Measurement leads to progress.

$

In trading, simplicity is the ultimate sophistication.

$

The fascinating thing about successful trading is that the right behaviors begin as written rules and evolve into habits.

$

Tracking your trading activities leads to growth and better results.

$

Strive to connect with seasoned and trustworthy traders, individuals who have forged a path of consistent success.

$

A losing trade shouldn't disturb you.

$

Do not be bothered by a loss; maintain the belief and conviction to bounce back.

$

Adapt to accepting small, managed losses. Regard them as essential steps, not disappointments.

$

Master traders exhibit discipline, focus, and confidence even in challenging situations, trusting their edge and themselves.

$

Becoming fixated on market analysis may create a perception of certitude.

$

Escaping excessive risks is vital for successful trading.

$

Strong motivation is a shared trait among high achievers, including successful traders.

$

To minimize the significance of a single trade, focus on the net outcome of the next ten or twenty trades.

$

Finding your trading niche is crucial to success in the markets.

$

Many traders get stuck trying to figure out why a trading instrument should go up or down. By the time it's clear, the move is almost done.

$

Focus on doing more of what works and less of what doesn't.

$

In trading, wisdom lies in amplifying what works and minimizing what doesn't.

$

Learn from your trading experience, but access quality trading resources and study successful traders.

$

Success demands a minimum level of experience, knowledge, and skill.

$

Proficiency in any endeavor demands time and experience. Be patient; results will come.

$

Set predefined drawdown limits to determine if a system is not performing as expected and should be discontinued.

$

Survival in trading demands adaptation, evolution, competition, or else extinction.

$

Assuming market behavior persists is a common mistake; be vigilant as markets can unexpectedly change.

$

A common mistake is assuming recent market behavior will persist, disregarding the changing nature of markets.

$

Discovering a consistent edge is the key to running a successful trading business.

$

Trade within your emotional capacity; avoid taking positions larger than you can handle.

$

Traders adhere to rules long-term if they align with their individual trading style.

$

Trading is a competition; ignite the competitor within you.

$

Your advantage doesn't disappear overnight. Negative signs build up slowly until they can't be ignored.

$

If your trading position keeps you up at night, it's time to let it go.

$

Trading for excitement is the most expensive form of speculation.

$

Chasing every price fluctuation is a futile endeavor with no chance of success.

$

Once you have a winning system in place and adhere to wise risk management, the only thing left to conquer is your own mentality.

$

Trading is a never-ending chain of dilemmas.

$

The essence of trading discipline lies in the absence of exceptions - none can be permitted.

$

Trading may seem deceptively simple, yet it remains one of the most challenging pursuits.

$

Be wary of overconfidence, as the largest profits are often followed by the biggest losses.

$

To trade successfully, focus on winning rather than being preoccupied with avoiding losses.

$

The three keys to good trading: Avoid averaging losers, size positions appropriately, and take regular profits.

$

Winning trades often show strength from the beginning.

$

Only invest what you can afford to lose without sacrificing your peace of mind.

$

When you find yourself hoping for a position to come back, reduce your size or close it.

$

Experience is the bare minimum requirement for success in trading.

$

Exceptional traders thrive on uncovering market advantages through continuous research and development.

$

Overanalyzing markets may provide an illusion of confidence.

$

Only put in the market what won't keep you up at night.

$

Novice traders expect every trade to win, while professionals anticipate the possibility of losses.

$

Uncertainty is an ineradicable feature of speculative markets.

$

The Profit Factor is the ultimate metric for ranking trading strategies, measuring dollar inflow versus dollar outflow.

$

To make money in trading, an organized trading plan is essential.

$

The art of discretionary trading entails finding a balance between the determination to pursue your ideas and the humility to accept when you are incorrect.

$

Quality and truth outweigh quantity in trading knowledge.

$

Recording your trades is vital for assessing your progress and enhancing your outcomes. It establishes a constant reference to unveil concealed patterns and imperfections in your performance.

$

Full-time commitment is key to successful trading.

$

Belief in the positive nature of money is crucial for accumulating wealth.

$

View money as a positive tool to add value and improve lives.

$

The path to ruin in trading is paved with the decision to keep adding to a losing position.

$

One of the most critical skills in trading is knowing when to stay out of the market.

$

Limiting losses: The vital cornerstone of trading.

$

For a trader, their capital is akin to inventory. Once it is gone, the business cannot continue.

$

The presence of stress in trading is an indicator that something is not quite right.

$

When you find your trading niche, the right actions become effortless.

$

Trading, like any business, demands a well-crafted trading plan to guide decision-making and operational activities in order to achieve success.

$

Reviewing your trading activity consistently is the path to growth and improvement as a trader.

$

Set goals and envision yourself achieving them.

$

The temptation to recoup all of your losses in a single trade is a recipe for failure in the markets.

$

Achieving maximum success in trading requires gradually increasing position sizes as your account grows, although this endeavor is not devoid of discomfort.

$

Do not forget that you do not need to make money on your current trade to generate profits in the markets.

$

To become a great trader, first, you must believe it's within you.

$

If you can see yourself reaching your goals, you are more likely to make them a reality.

$

Believing in your capabilities is crucial for success.

$

Simplicity is key in trading. Adding complexity will only hinder your success.

$

Successful trading requires detachment from money.

$

Right trading behaviors transition from written rules to habits and eventually become core trading beliefs.

$

Developing traders can enhance performance by mentally rehearsing rules, journaling, and using affirmations like "follow your rules" on post-it notes. Repetition internalizes these messages, becoming natural in a trader's self-talk.

$

A great trader adapts to changing markets.

$

Seasoned traders remain unfazed by a series of losses and maintain rule-based discipline.

$

In trading, you either play for the thrill or for the win.

$

If you cannot articulate your trading methodology, avoid putting your hard-earned money at risk in the markets.

$

Without a methodology, you're just gambling, and that's a sure way to lose your hard-earned money.

$

The path to discovering an edge is to locate entry points with a probability greater than average of the market moving in the desired direction within a specific timeframe.

$

You are your own biggest limitation in trading. Keep developing.

$

Backtesting trading systems requires experience and skill.

$

Focus on doing the right things, not on single trading outcomes.

$

To become a consistently winning short-term trader, how long should you persevere? Until you succeed!

$

Proper backtesting requires a deep understanding of the market and experience. Beginners often overlook important details that can lead to costly mistakes.

$

Mistakes are an inevitable part of trading, just as they are in life.

$

The greats in any field are always learning.

$

Mistakes are inevitable. Similar to top athletes, traders need a resilient mindset to bounce back without losing composure.

$

Traders, like athletes, must have a winning attitude to succeed.

$

Elite traders embrace a winning attitude, learning from mistakes and using setbacks as fuel for growth, propelling them forward.

$

Resist the temptation to alter a trading system merely due to a few consecutive losing trades.

$

Trading is not a job. It's a scalable business.

$

Sticking to a plan can be hard, especially when the market isn't behaving the way we want it to.

$

The best traders know that success is a long game. They understand that one or two losing trades don't mean their system is flawed.

$

Don't touch a stock or future that spooks you. Your instincts are warning you for a reason.

$

Trading requires constant self-improvement just like any high-performance activity.

$

The more a trader prepares, the better their results will be.

$

Learning is a never-ending journey, especially for elite performers.

$

The best traders know that data is their friend, and that a data-driven approach is the key to success.

$

Small trading edges require flawless execution; otherwise, a winning system can quickly turn into a losing one.

$

Even the tiniest advantage can mean the difference between profit and loss. But here's the catch - execution is everything.

$

Anticipate bad luck and plan accordingly.

$

Edges are small, execution is everything, and the line between success and failure is razor-thin.

$

Sticking to a trading system over an extended period necessitates cultivating a high level of discipline.

$

Regardless of the market or the time frame, there is always a path to profitability, and it is your responsibility to uncover it.

$

In less mature and less crowded markets, stronger and cleaner trends tend to emerge.

$

The successful trades are often the ones that start in the money.

$

You can have the best system in the world, but if you don't execute flawlessly, it won't matter.

$

To counteract doubt and uncertainty in the markets, develop a systematic trading process.

$

Strictly managing losses is vital for successful trading.

$

True trading confidence stems from dedication and the accumulation of practical knowledge and expertise.

$

Overtrading creates a problem by pushing the trader out of their niche, their performance zone.

$

A trade that yields profit due to ill-advised decisions isn't a triumph; it's a looming hazard.

$

Mastering trading requires proficiency in both technical and tactical aspects—knowing how and when to trade.

$

It is a common tendency amongst traders to repeat the same mistakes over and over again until the lesson is finally learned.

$

When armed with a winning system and a measured approach to risk management, the only obstacle is your mindset.

$

If you manage risk and follow a positive expectancy model, trading should be unexciting.

$

Many desire the trader's life - wealth, freedom, location independence. But, it takes years of devotion, losses, and transformation to achieve. Dream is simple, reality is hard.

$

Trades with high chance of success follow the trend. Market participants believe in the trend direction.

$

Smart, knowledgeable, patient traders will always have a bright future.

$

Staring at prices all day is like constantly feeding a slot machine.

$

Never ever adjust a stop loss to allow for more leeway.

$

Professional traders focus on doing the right thing, not just on making money.

$

Successful trading starts with knowing your core strengths and weaknesses.

$

Avoid entering a subpar trade merely out of a need for activity or excitement.

$

Concentrate on doing the right thing, not on the unpredictable outcome of individual trades.

$

To become a consistent winner in trading, keep trying until you succeed!

$

New traders lack the experience and skills necessary for proper historical testing.

$

If your strategy involves getting stopped out often but remaining profitable, it's easier to accept being stopped out.

$

Exceptional athletes and traders possess a winning attitude that enables them to overcome mistakes and persevere.

$

A trader should embody the strategic foresight of a chess player, the precision of a sniper, and the rhythmic skill of a musician.

$

When you can fully enjoy your personal time without checking the market or your profits, you've become a master trader.

$

When executed effectively, scalping can serve as a powerful trading strategy. Never underestimate the importance of scoring many small wins while maintaining consistency.

$

Becoming a trader involves more than just learning trading techniques. It's a personal growth journey over several years.

$

In all areas of elite performance, performers review their work to continue learning.

$

Simplifying means removing what's unnecessary, allowing the essential to be heard.

$

Avoid setting daily profit targets and focus on long-term performance goals for greater consistency.

$

Believe you're a pro trader and strive to think and act like one every single day.

$

Experience the magic of programming your subconscious by setting written goals.

$

Many people can't become traders as they struggle to embrace uncertainty.

$

To stay closely aligned with the markets, eliminate phrases like "I think," "I disagree," and "In my opinion" from your thought process.

$

The mental strength gained from the process of becoming a successful trader will transform your life beyond trading.

$

Unsuccessful traders tend to delay accepting losses.

$

The process of becoming a successful trader cultivates mental strength that extends far beyond trading, transforming your life.

$

If you truly enjoy trading, you'll stick with it for the long haul and excel. Success and money will follow.

$

Monday is the favorite day of the week for successful young traders.

$

Your previous failures don't define you. Instead, they equip you for future triumphs.

$

Don't try to dig yourself out of a losing day by taking excessive risks to break even.

$

It's possible to experience a day of losses while still ending the week with profits.

$

Extreme emotions manifest as price action, resulting in high volatility in the market.

$

Becoming a successful trader requires unwavering belief that it's the only path meant for you.

$

All traders experience tough times. It's crucial to learn how to handle and navigate through them.

$

Trading, when done right, leads to a better life, freedom, and financial independence.

$

To succeed in markets, you need two things: find a trading advantage and execute it flawlessly.

$

To become proficient in trading, like any profession, you need time and experience.

$

As a trader, you have the privilege of earning income with a mere click from your home's comfort. Embrace and appreciate this opportunity.

$

Gain an advantage through thorough market research.

$

Valuable discoveries arise from unsuccessful positions in trading.

$

When winning, you're vulnerable to mistakes like overtrading, taking big positions, breaking rules, or lacking prudence.

$

If something is profitable, it simply works.

$

Successful trading is not about being excited; it's about maintaining a calm and composed emotional state.

$

Your unique way of thinking and your strengths should be reflected in what and how you trade.

$

The opposite of excitement is the emotional state linked to successful trading.

$

Every highly successful trader is exceptionally original in their market approach.

$

Probabilities offer insight, yet they don't encompass everything, given the continuous emergence of new scenarios.

$

Trading approaches must constantly evolve based on changing market conditions; they can't remain static indefinitely.

$

The journey to consistent trading is tough, but the rewards make it worthwhile: financial gains and personal fulfillment.

$

Even the most successful traders experience losses. How they handle and manage themselves during those times makes a significant difference in their ability to bounce back.

$

When a trader is losing, they often hide their losses from others and themselves, often in denial.

$

Bad trading habits can resurface when you become tired, lazy, or careless; you're never immune to them.

$

If you lack confidence, fear will be present to some extent.

$

The emotional state that characterizes successful trading is the polar opposite of excitement.

$

Our psychology is influenced by trading just as trading is influenced by our psychology.

$

Get a notebook, jot down market observations; it sparks ideas and helps you cultivate trading habits.

$

The top performers generate superior ideas because they generate a multitude of ideas.

$

When we strongly identify with a trading style or analysis, we tend to close ourselves off to alternatives.

$

To master our trading future, we must accept that the present is temporary and subject to change.

$

In intraday trading, it's crucial to avoid trading when no advantage is perceived for a trading edge.

$

Trading advantages don't vanish suddenly. Negative signs accumulate slowly until they can't be ignored anymore.

$

When you make multiple daily trades, it's relatively simple to track the quality of your trading advantage.

$

Trades are only meaningful within a strong system that is consistently applied with discipline and risk management.

$

Successful traders focus on self-improvement as much as market analysis, developing routines to optimize decision-making states.

$

By noting small observations of the market, you'll generate numerous trading ideas.

$

Be ruthless in discarding anything without an edge. If unsure, an indicator or setup lacks an edge—purge it!

$

My style is earning small profits frequently—a defining characteristic of my trading approach.

$

No one cares for your money and future like you do.

$

Persistent trading failure signals underlying problems that need to be addressed.

$

To thrive as a trader, adaptation to evolving markets is essential in the long run.

$

Perceiving market patterns is one key trading skill, crucial for success.

$

Traders often fear losing profits and take sure gains when signs of a reversal appear.

$

Many traders treat trading casually like a hobby, but hobbies often incur costs.

$

People often fail to follow either part of this rule due to biases: cutting losses short and letting profits run.

$

Frequent trading often lowers profit odds; the most selective traders are usually the best.

$

Speculating means taking risks with favorable odds, while gambling involves risks with unfavorable odds.

$

A top trader maintains optimal brain condition for peak performance.

$

Market success is about always finding new advantages in changing markets, not sticking rigidly to just one way.

$

If your results are unsatisfactory, don't repeat the same actions. Analyze your mistakes and make adjustments.

$

Successful traders don't overly emphasize any single trade's significance.

$

Inconsistent buying and selling in similar situations indicate a serious discipline issue.

$

Success comes from trading with your own perspective and gaining confidence in your approach.

$

To overcome overtrading, redirect activity towards creative and constructive trading directions.

$

Rare and valuable is the ability to observe the market without deviating from your trading plan.

$

Avoid the detrimental mental state of believing the market owes you something after consecutive losses.

$

Resolve your worst trading losses when they are still small and insignificant.

$

The key predictor of trading success is the preparation-to-trading time ratio.

$

Your path to successful future trading involves maintaining a continuous source of potential new trading edges to utilize.

$

Trading is relatively simple, but the challenging part lies in the research, design, coding, testing, and implementation processes.

$

Your goal is to ensure your family remains unaware of your daily trading results, reflecting ultimate emotional control.

$

Achieving success in trading requires putting in just as much effort into self-improvement as you do into understanding the markets. It's a vital part of the journey to success that you shouldn't overlook.

$

Maintain a steady mindset regardless of winning or losing on the day.

$

Steer clear of scenarios where risk cannot be effectively managed.

$

Exceptional traders always seek new advantages, continuously researching and developing strategies.

$

Markets repeat patterns. The game is trading these patterns. Experience makes it easier.

$

Believing in your consistency is crucial for accumulating wealth as a trader.

$

Maintain daily trade notes, recording results and emotions for reflection and improvement.

$

Backtesting reveals the past performance of your trading setup, clarifying your approach and exposing flaws.

$

Inability to accept small losses leads to potential catastrophic losses in the future.

$

Accepting 8 to 10 consecutive trading losses yearly is essential; safeguard your account during these times.

$

Paper trading can't fully prepare you for the real market's emotional and financial pressures.

$

Perseverance, discernment, and opportune timing are pivotal for trader success.

$

Many of a trader's worst trades result from impulsive actions driven by a desire to act.

$

The trading journal serves as a valuable tool for monitoring and understanding our actions in trading.

$

Many traders use ineffective tools, like complex technical indicators, without realizing their inefficacy.

$

Your previous trading mistakes don't define you. Instead, they equip you for future triumphs.

$

Volume and volatility go hand in hand. They are closely connected.

$

In the markets, you have control over two variables: when you participate and how much you invest.

$

Refusing to acknowledge mistakes prevents growth and hinders becoming a skilled trader.

$

The mental strength you cultivate as a successful trader will profoundly impact your life beyond trading.

$

A select few achieved vast riches through keen attention to overlooked details.

$

In trading, a day may be lost, but the week can be profitable.

$

Successful traders possess a distinctive perspective that allows them to perceive markets uniquely.

$

Awareness of edge failure risk is crucial for effective market navigation.

$

Your trading quality is a blend of system quality and execution ability.

$

Traders are intellectual athletes.

$

Optimization's value lies in setting broad parameter boundaries for a system.

$

Fine-tuning optimization is often a futile effort or even self-deception.

$

Remaining calm after a loss is vital for trading success.

$

Financial freedom relies on your spending habits.

$

Chasing a monetary target leads to undesired trades.

$

Impeccable work ethic yields remarkable rewards.

$

Trading becomes easier when you don't rely on it for financial needs.

$

Impeccable work ethic yields remarkable rewards.

$

While science provides valuable inputs, trading is an art form.

$

Money is drawn to those with positive thoughts and feelings about it.

$

Avoid being overly curious about all the reasons behind price movements, as it can cloud your judgment. Simply acknowledge the move and capitalize on it.

$

Successful traders seldom have an effortless journey, except when they hail from a family of traders.

$

Trading wisdom is cultivated through experience, not age.

$

If you neglect developing your trading edge, others will compete for your money by honing theirs.

$

It takes years of learning about the market to figure out what information you can ignore.

$

In trading, the impossible happens approximately twice a year.

$

As a discretionary trader, seeking someone else's opinion on a trade is a sign to exit your position.

$

When you base your trading decisions on information beyond your established strategy, you introduce random factors that can disrupt your trading system.

$

The key to being a great trader, and a significant challenge for many, is patiently waiting for the right trading setup.

$

Forget complex indicators and fancy technical tools. Instead, concentrate on what works in the current market you're trading.

$

Traders' success stems from not assigning excessive importance to any individual trade.

$

Avoid trading when you can't afford to lose.

$

A trading edge is simply a signal of a greater likelihood of one outcome over another.

$

Don't exceed your comfort level when betting. Take your time until you're prepared.

$

If small losses bother you, explore other interests.

$

Evaluate the robustness of your trading system by comparing short-term metrics with their long-term counterparts.

$

You can achieve remarkable things by persisting and not giving up.

$

Even the most accomplished traders face periods of loss. How they handle both their losses and themselves during these times can significantly impact their ability to make a swift comeback.

$

Avoid using the phrase "dollars per day" from now on.

$

No strategy is superior, only the one that suits you best.

$

Extensive understanding of the trading concept and its behavior across market conditions reduces the reliance on historical testing.

$

After losing money, resist rushing; maintain focus and strategy for better outcomes.

$

Learn from your trades; the sole path to progress.

$

Trading styles often breed toxicity. Intraday and swing traders believe in their superiority, as do momentum and mean-reversion traders.

$

Forget about the money and focus on the process.

$

Focus solely on your trading system; ignore everything else.

$

A common trait among successful trades is their understanding that losses are inherent to the game, and they've all acquired the skill of embracing losses.

$

Go into the trade expecting nothing.

$

True trading success and consistency arise only when you can fully trust yourself to cut losses on losing trades.

$

The finest traders have mastered the skill of handling losses.

$

If you believe something cannot occur, you just haven't experienced enough yet.

$

In trading, more than money is at risk. Your self-worth, confidence, and future are on the line too.

$

Creating systems that offset your own harmful impulses is the essence of successful trading.

$

It's not finding the statistical advantage that's tough, but being emotionally stable and consistent in capitalizing on it.

$

Those who excel as day traders are elite achievers who have earned mastery.

$

Successful trading doesn't have a one-size-fits-all approach or answer.

$

Bad trades are common. Your future success depends on how you handle them.

$

It is impossible to prevent pain by avoiding trading losses.

$

Markets have various personalities, and strategies that succeed with one may fail with another.

$

A trading irony: winning trades often leave you feeling unsatisfied, either because you didn't stay in long enough or your position size was too small.

$

In successful trading, a crucial principle is that straying from established rules constitutes an error. Furthermore, lacking these written rules renders every action a mistake.

$

If you stick to one path until you achieve success in trading, you develop expertise. If you pursue multiple strategies simultaneously, you won't master any.

$

Trading and life are deeply interconnected. The more you comprehend yourself, the greater the probability of discovering a trading instrument, a system, or an overall trading philosophy that aligns with your personality.

$

Markets have various personalities, and strategies that succeed with one may fail with another.

$

Trading a setup is a rational way to trade, aiding you in battling the emotions traders often face.

$

You must be mindful that a very bad trade can wipe out months or even years of profits.

$

To become a professional trader, you need a trading edge that elevates you from the rest of the losing crowd.

$

Experiencing trading success when no one believed in you feels extraordinary.

$

As an introvert, I chose trading because it allows me to work alone. Success or failure is solely up to me.

$

The markets entice and are unforgiving to those who lack strength and discipline.

$

Becoming a professional trader requires gaining a trading edge, the weapon that sets you apart from the wandering flock.

$

Skillful traders thrive on uncertainty.

$

Even if I teach a trader one of my best setups, they will start adjusting it to suit their trading style, especially after a series of consecutive losses.

$

Traders who have mastered the skill of consistency can seize the chance to establish a life of independence.

$

Copying others won't yield lasting success.

$

Traders often learn a bit about different styles but keep seeking new methods. Switching too much resets your learning curve.

$

One of the concealed keys to making a living from trading is to trade smarter and less frequently.

$

Selling prematurely does not exist; rather, it signifies a lack of a systematic approach for exiting profitable trades.

$

Your impulsive trading decisions may serve as a significant obstacle in your pursuit of trading for a living.

$

Once you enter a trade, your objectivity declines instantly and in direct proportion to the trade's size.

$

Lacking self-trust as a trader ensures no chance of success.

$

Without proper risk management in trading, all other efforts become inconsequential. Ultimately, any profits gained will be surrendered in the long run.

$

Much of the emotional frustration and disruption in trading arise from attempting to force-fit markets into a preferred framework, instead of discovering the framework that best describes market behavior.

$

Strive to become the trader focused on making money over time, rather than the one desperate to be right immediately.

$

The more you engage in reading, research, and study, the more proficient you'll become as a trader. Continuous learning is rewarded in trading.

$

Flourishing in trading demands solitary dedication to self-growth—crafting skills, bolstering confidence, and shaping a personal, reliable winning strategy.

$

Staring at price quotes won't alter the market's trajectory. Passion for your work is essential to excel in any profession.

$

Seeking inspiration for your unique trading approach? Observe the market, jot in your journal. Gather, curate, and evolve your strategies.

$

New traders usually lack a good strategy and don't grasp risk. It's normal for them to lose some small accounts as they learn.

$

Crafting a profitable strategy requires identifying market causality. Study aftermath: observe patterns following events.

$

Frame your market research elegantly: Pose questions about market behavior, delve into historical data for answers.

$

As a trader, keep seeking "what if" ideas. If the market behaves a certain way, what's likely to follow? This quest uncovers unique trading edges.

$

Flow occurs when you're so focused on an activity that time slips away. This state drives elite performance across fields like sports, trading, and writing.

$

Experienced testers effectively narrow research focus, gaining concise, valuable trading insights.

$

In the trading world, there's a strong desire for markets to be completely measurable, with an appetite for certainty. Some individuals even entertain the idea that there's an inherent truth akin to natural laws hidden within trading patterns.

$

Recognize that accepting a minor loss carries no shame.

$

Winning traders possess a meticulously crafted process, the discipline to follow it, and an unwavering dedication to relentless refinement.

$

From a couple of hundred backtests, only one or two may demonstrate effectiveness and be applied to real-money trading.

$

Through backtesting experience, you'll grasp market subtleties, guiding future research. The longer you test, the more familiar you become with market tendencies.

$

In trading, focus on executing trades flawlessly. After a set of trades, assess gains. Obsessing over account value leads to mistakes and failure.

$

Great traders adjust to changes. They notice what's happening in the market and change their strategies to match.

$

Have you strayed from your plan due to impulses? Avoid by logging trades with strategy labels.

$

Although the process of analyzing markets and price movements is commonly referred to as market research, I prefer to liken it to the pursuit of uncovering valuable treasures.

$

Understanding a technical indicator fully isn't sufficient for market success. I've seen traders who know indicators well but can't profit. Deep indicator knowledge is useless if misapplied to unsuitable markets.

$

Amateurs evade trading losses, while experts manage them.

$

Incompetent traders tend to perceive themselves as infallible, consistently placing blame on the market for any perceived inaccuracies.

$

In the realm of trading, money serves merely as a tool—a means to keep score.

$

Your success hinges on your ability to follow your signals as much as the signals themselves.

$

Ensure your signals align with your schedule and life commitments; this is crucial for success.

$

A trader who only goes by their emotions and ignores a plan is definitely going to lose.

$

An inexperienced trader is uncertain about how to react when circumstances turn against them.

$

A gap will persist between the real and ideal trader—the one you are and the one you can become.

$

Your goal is to become a trader who stays calm and composed.

$

Winning traders discover a competitive advantage and then work hard to make it even better.

$

Making sound trading decisions becomes challenging when you're tired or stressed.

$

Completing a log sheet for each trade you make is one method to prevent impulsive trades.

$

Paper trading is beneficial for practicing execution and getting familiar with a new trading platform.

$

Without real money at risk, a trader won't grasp how to perform under pressure.

$

Increasing your trading size is much like building muscle with weights.

$

Gradually, you'll adapt to larger dollar fluctuations in your trading account.

$

Over time, you must become accustomed to handling progressively larger amounts.

$

Quantified trading is recognizing that by executing a specific trade frequently, your edge will manifest.

$

Day traders don't need to concern themselves with whether we're in an inflationary or deflationary cycle.

$

Consider each trade as one of the next one hundred; does it significantly matter when viewed this way?

$

The ability to think innovatively and adaptability stand out as crucial indicators for achieving long-term success in trading.

$

The more you test, the greater the chance for good luck to intervene, as you have more opportunities to encounter something that aligns well with the market you are studying.

$

The finest traders have been utilizing the same setup in the same market for many years. They disregard everything else.

$

Understand the factors behind a system's poor performance.

$

The pivotal stride toward becoming a prosperous trader lies in mastering the art of acknowledging losses without succumbing to anger or frustration.

$

Market conditions shift periodically. The true skill for a trader lies in recognizing when to adjust, fine-tune a system, or discard it altogether to construct a new one.

$

It's much easier to be more aggressive with accumulated profits.

$

Predicting the future is an impossible task.

$

The largest drawdowns typically occur when the market conditions change.

$

Traders need to recognize that they cannot sustain a livelihood by trading the news from any financial news channel.

$

Success can involve frequent or infrequent trading. Stable, consistent, top-performing systems are overtly simplistic.

$

I've crafted enduringly profitable systems, some untouched for over 5 years. Minimal parameter adjustments maintained others. Simplicity and robustness drive their design.

$

Engaging in activities and hobbies beyond trading helps traders gain perspective, reduce stress, and manage their emotions more effectively.

$

Human nature often leads us to doubt ourselves, but our potential far exceeds our doubts. To become a great trader, you must first believe in the potential within you.

$

The journey to trading success is not a linear path.

$

There is no greater satisfaction than mastering the markets.

***

Chapter 4

Enhancing Trading and Life through Non-Trading Beliefs

The beliefs a person gathers throughout life end up shaping many of their experiences. When it comes to trading, beliefs about life in general, especially regarding money and its nature, or self-worth and self-esteem, determine abundance beyond a certain level of technical and tactical development. Over the years, I've been jotting down my key beliefs and ideas in a small Moleskine notebook, often drawn from the thoughts of philosophers, self-help books, literature, or even interviews, and later refined to fit my own context. The following are the ones I consider most important for accumulating wealth through trading:

$

Anyone can attain wealth.

$

Your spending habits determine financial freedom.

$

Avoid caffeine 8-10 hours before going to sleep.

$

Take care of your rest and nutrition.

$

Choosing to feel positive is your essential daily decision.

$

Comfort makes you weaker.

$

Success starts after envy stops.

$

A morning walk is meditation in motion, clearing your mind.

$

Embrace deserving money. Pursue boldly.

$

Your son deserves your greatness.

$

You deserve to win because you're the best-prepared trader in your niche.

$

Not exercising means you're not as clever as you believe.

$

Without an obsession for it, mastery will forever elude you.

$

The key to becoming an expert is simple: keep trying, don't give up.

$

A strong work ethic leads to success.

$

Quality relationships, especially marriage, impact trading. Support from partner matters due to trading's non-linear income, preventing issues during ups and downs.

$

Peak experiences energize marriages; absence erodes. Invest in enriching experiences, from dating to travel, to sustain family well-being.

$

Use written goals to program your subconscious.
Experience the magic.

$

Treat people well without a reason.

$

It's alright to win.

$

The outcomes you desire often lie merely one belief apart.

$

No one's concern matches yours for your wealth and future.

THE END

Appendix I

Journey to Profits: Navigating the Phases of Trading Success

Understand your progress toward steady profitability.

There are five key phases leading to consistent profitability. Which stage do you find yourself in?

I. The initial phase is marked by frequent significant losses. New traders often lack understanding, mistakenly believing they know enough—an especially perilous mindset that threatens both accounts and emotional well-being.

II. In the second phase, traders address recurring errors, resulting in smaller losses. Though a hit-or-miss approach still predominates, lessons from previous losses temper the impact, increasing trader resilience.

III. The subsequent phase features a trader familiar with technicalities, stock trends, and renowned trading literature. Generally break-even, avoiding losses is an essential step toward eventual success.

IV. Upon encountering valuable resources, traders gain independence, analyze personalized data, and adopt a more selective trading style. Consistently profitable but experiencing occasional significant downturns, true stability remains elusive.

V. Achieving consistent wins, traders tailor strategies, master mental skills, and trade effortlessly. Unconcerned with others' opinions, they may even find amusement in market calls. A rarity, this phase offers the potential for trading as a profession. Such traders recognize their accomplishment.

Glossary

Equity curve. A visual representation of the cumulative performance of an investment or trading strategy over time, showing the change in account balance.

Trading system. A structured set of rules and parameters designed to guide the execution of buying and selling financial instruments, aiming to achieve specific trading goals or strategies.

Self-Sabotage. The act of undermining one's own goals, success, or well-being through deliberate or subconscious actions, behaviors, or thought patterns.

Edge (trading edge). An advantage or unique approach that gives a trader a higher probability of making profitable trades over the long term, often based on strategies, analysis, or insights that others may not possess.

Trading philosophy. A trader's core beliefs, principles, and approach to financial markets, which guide their decision-making, risk management, and overall trading strategy.

Learning curve. The gradual process of gaining expertise and improving trading skills over time through experience, practice, and learning from both successes and failures in financial markets.

Trading niche. A specialized and focused area within the financial markets where a trader concentrates their efforts, often based on specific assets, strategies, or market segments, in order to develop expertise and gain a competitive advantage.

Drawdown (Trading): The reduction in a trader's account value from its peak level to its lowest point, often expressed as a percentage, representing the extent of losses experienced during a specific trading period or strategy.

Profit Factor: A financial metric used in trading that calculates the ratio of gross profits to gross losses. It provides a measure of the profitability and risk-reward ratio of a trading strategy or system, with higher values indicating more profitable trading.

Financial Freedom: The state of having sufficient wealth, assets, and financial resources to live the desired lifestyle and cover expenses without the need for active employment or dependence on others, affording individuals the freedom to make choices and pursue their goals without financial constraints.

Discretionary Trading: A trading approach where investment decisions, such as buying or selling financial assets, are made based on the trader's subjective judgment, experience, and analysis, rather than following predefined rules or algorithms. It involves a high degree of personal discretion and interpretation of market conditions.

Backtesting (Trading Research): The process of evaluating the performance of a trading strategy or model by applying it to historical market data to simulate how it would have performed in the past. This helps traders assess its potential effectiveness and make informed decisions about its future use in live trading.

Risk Management (Short-Term Trading): The systematic approach of identifying, assessing, and mitigating potential financial losses in short-term trading activities by implementing strategies, position sizing, and stop-loss orders to protect capital and minimize the impact of adverse market movements.

Systematic Trading: A method of trading in financial markets where investment decisions are based on predefined rules and algorithms, often relying on quantitative analysis and automated trading systems. It aims to remove emotional bias and subjectivity from trading by relying on systematic, data-driven strategies.

Overtrading: A behavior in trading where a trader engages in excessive buying and selling of financial assets. It can lead to increased transaction costs, greater exposure to losses, and reduced overall profitability.

Stop Loss. An order placed by a trader to automatically sell a financial asset when its price reaches a specified level, designed to limit potential losses by exiting a losing position before it incurs further decline.

Daily Profit Target: A predetermined monetary objective that short-term traders set for themselves to achieve within a single trading day.

Market Volatility: The degree of variation and fluctuation in the prices of financial assets, such as stocks, currencies, or commodities, over a specific period of time. High market volatility indicates rapid and significant price movements, while low volatility suggests relatively stable and slower price changes. Traders often analyze volatility to assess the level of risk in the market. Various factors, including economic events, geopolitical developments, and market sentiment, can influence market volatility.

Market Conditions: The current state of financial markets, influenced by factors such as supply and demand, economic indicators, geopolitics, investor sentiment, and technical aspects like price trends and volatility. Traders and investors analyze these conditions to guide their asset-related decisions, with market conditions ranging from stability and bullish sentiment to uncertainty and heightened volatility. Adapting to changing market conditions is vital for effective trading and risk management.

Market Research: The systematic process of collecting, analyzing, and interpreting relevant data and information about financial markets, assets, or securities. Effective market research is crucial for developing trading strategies, managing risk, and achieving success in financial markets.

Intraday Trading: A trading strategy in which financial instruments, such as stocks, currencies, or commodities, are bought and sold within the same trading day. Intraday traders seek to profit from short-term price movements and typically do not hold positions overnight. This approach involves frequent trading, often taking advantage of small price fluctuations throughout the trading session.

Market Patterns: Recognizable and repeatable formations or sequences of price and volume movements in financial markets.

Paper Trading: A simulation or practice trading technique in which traders or investors execute hypothetical trades using fictitious or "paper" money instead of real capital. Paper trading allows individuals to test their trading strategies, assess their skills, and gain experience in a risk-free environment. It involves tracking and recording trades and their outcomes as if they were real, providing valuable insights into potential trading performance without the actual financial risk. It is often used for educational purposes, strategy development, and to build confidence before committing real funds to the market.

Trading Journal: A systematic record-keeping tool used by traders and investors to document and analyze their trading activities. A trading journal typically includes details such as the date and time of each trade, the financial instrument traded, the trade entry and exit prices, position size, trading strategy employed, reasons for entering or exiting a trade, and the outcome of the trade (profit or loss). Additionally, traders often include notes on their emotions, market conditions, and any lessons learned during the trading session. Maintaining a trading journal helps individuals evaluate their trading performance, identify strengths and weaknesses, and refine their strategies. It is a valuable tool for improving trading skills and decision-making over time.

Technical Indicators: Quantitative tools and calculations applied to historical price and volume data of financial assets, primarily used by traders and analysts for making informed trading decisions. Technical indicators help assess market trends, momentum, volatility, and potential buy or sell signals. These indicators are plotted on charts and can take various forms, including moving averages, oscillators (e.g., Relative Strength Index - RSI, Stochastic Oscillator), and trend-following indicators (e.g., Moving Average Convergence Divergence - MACD). Traders use technical indicators to gain insights into market conditions, identify potential entry and exit points, and develop trading strategies based on historical price patterns and statistical analysis.

Volume: A key quantitative measure in financial markets that represents the total number of shares, contracts, or units of a financial instrument traded within a specific time period, such as a trading day, hour, or minute. Volume is an essential indicator of market activity and liquidity, helping traders and analysts assess the level of buying and selling interest in a particular asset.

Optimization: The process of systematically refining and adjusting trading strategies, risk management techniques to achieve better performance, efficiency, or desired outcomes. In trading, optimization often involves tweaking various parameters within a trading system or algorithm to maximize profits, minimize risks, or enhance overall trading results. Traders may use historical data and backtesting to identify optimal settings for their strategies. Optimization is a continuous and data-driven practice aimed at improving trading performance and adapting to changing market conditions.

Trading Size: The specific quantity or position size of a financial instrument (such as shares of stock, future contracts) that a trader or investor buys or sells in a single trade. Trading size is a critical parameter in trading decisions, as it determines the level of exposure to market risk and the potential profit or loss on a trade. Properly managing trading size is essential for risk control and aligning a trading strategy with one's risk tolerance and financial objectives. Traders often adjust their trading size based on factors like account size, volatility, and the perceived risk of a particular trade.

Trading Setup: A predefined set of conditions, criteria, or signals that traders use to identify potential trading opportunities in financial markets. A trading setup typically involves a combination of technical and/or fundamental analysis factors that, when met, suggest that a specific trade may be favorable. These factors can include price patterns, technical indicators, economic news events, or other market signals. Traders rely on trading setups to guide their entry and exit decisions, helping them systematically identify and act upon potential trades based on their chosen trading strategy and objectives.

Mean Reversion Trading: A short-term trading strategy that capitalizes on the belief that asset prices tend to oscillate around their historical average or mean levels. Mean reversion traders look for assets that have temporarily moved away from this mean, either due to overbought (prices above the mean) or oversold (prices below the mean) conditions. They expect the price to revert back to the mean, creating trading opportunities. Traders using this strategy typically take short-term positions, aiming to profit from price corrections as the asset returns to its historical average. Mean reversion trading is often employed with the goal of capturing relatively small price movements within short timeframes.

Momentum Trading: A short-term trading strategy that focuses on identifying and capitalizing on existing price trends in financial markets. Momentum traders believe that assets that have been performing well (showing upward momentum) will continue to do so, while assets with poor performance (showing downward momentum) will continue in the same direction. These traders use technical indicators and chart patterns to identify assets exhibiting strong recent price movements. They then take short-term positions in the direction of the prevailing trend, aiming to profit from continued price momentum. Momentum trading typically involves shorter holding periods and relies on the principle that trends can persist for a brief period, offering opportunities for quick gains.

Swing Trading: A short- to medium-term trading strategy that seeks to capitalize on price "swings" or fluctuations in financial markets. Swing traders aim to identify and profit from price movements within a given trend or range-bound market. They typically hold positions for several days to weeks, as opposed to day traders who enter and exit positions within a single trading day. Swing traders use a combination of technical analysis, chart patterns, and other indicators to identify potential entry and exit points. This strategy aims to capture intermediate price movements while avoiding the noise of short-term market fluctuations, making it well-suited for traders looking for a balance between short-term and long-term trading approaches.

Trading Wisdom: A collective body of knowledge, insights, principles, and practical lessons derived from the experiences and expertise of seasoned traders and investors. Trading wisdom encompasses both technical and psychological aspects of trading, offering valuable guidance on risk management, strategy development, decision-making, and emotional discipline. It often consists of time-tested strategies, rules of thumb, and pearls of wisdom that traders use to navigate the complexities and challenges of short-term trading successfully. Trading wisdom serves as a source of mentorship and guidance for traders, helping them make informed decisions and avoid common pitfalls in the fast-paced world of trading.

Trading Style: A trader's individual approach and methodology for conducting trades and making investment decisions. Trading style encompasses various aspects, including the frequency of trading (e.g., day trading, swing trading), the duration of trade holding periods (e.g., short-term, long-term), the types of financial instruments traded (e.g., stocks, forex, commodities), and the strategies employed (e.g., momentum trading, mean reversion trading). A trader's chosen style reflects their trading objectives, risk tolerance, and personal preferences. It serves as a blueprint for how they analyze markets, enter and exit positions, manage risk, and seek profit opportunities in the financial markets.

About the author:

Henrique M. Simões is a seasoned futures trader with over two decades of expertise in decoding the intricate world of short-term trading patterns. From the early stages of his career, Henrique was captivated by the dynamic nature of financial markets, leading him on a relentless pursuit of knowledge and mastery in the art of trading.

With a wealth of hands-on experience accumulated over 20-plus years, Henrique has honed his skills in navigating the complexities of the market, specializing in short-term trading strategies that require a keen understanding of market dynamics and swift decision-making. His unique insights into trading patterns have not only withstood the test of time but have consistently yielded success in the fast-paced world of futures trading.

Henrique M. Simões is not only a trader but also a dedicated educator. In his acclaimed work, "Trading Course: How to Become a Consistently Winning Trader," he shares the accumulated wisdom from his extensive journey in the financial markets. The book serves as a comprehensive guide for aspiring traders, offering practical insights, strategies, and the mindset necessary to achieve consistent success in the unpredictable realm of trading.

Known for his analytical acumen and strategic approach, Henrique continues to be a respected figure in the trading community. His commitment to excellence, coupled with a passion for sharing knowledge, has established him as a go-to resource for those seeking to thrive in the ever-evolving landscape of financial markets.

Whether in front of the trading screen or behind the pages of his insightful writings, Henrique M. Simões remains dedicated to empowering fellow traders with the tools and knowledge needed to navigate the challenges and opportunities presented by the dynamic world of futures trading.

Made in the USA
Monee, IL
02 August 2025